Bluegrass Fiddle
by Gene Lowinger

Oak Publications
New York • London • Tokyo • Sydney • Cologne

Acknowledgements

I would like to thank Mike Seeger for his assistance in compiling the historical material, and Ralph Rinzler for the discography material used in this book.

Photographs

Doug Connor: page 19, 26, 41, 48 and 58
Diana Davies: cover
David Gahr: page 8, 39, 56 and 62
Jean Hammons: page 31
Ira Haskell: page 9 and 10
Lindsay: page 7
David Weintraub: page 64

Book Design by Ira Haskell and Jean Hammons

e d c

©Oak Publications 1974

A Division of Embassy Music Corporation
All Rights Reserved

International Standard Book Number: 0-8256-0150-9
Library of Congress Catalog Card Number: 73-92395

Distributed throughout the world by Music Sales Corporation:

33 West 60th Street, New York 10023
78 Newman Street, London W1P 3LA
4-26-22 Jingumae, Shibuya-ku, Tokyo 150
27 Clarendon Street, Artarmon, Sydney NSW 2064
Kölner Strasse 199, D-5000, Cologne 90

Contents

Introduction	4
Musical Terminology	6
The Left Hand	8
The Right Hand	10
Old Joe Clark	12
Sally Goodin	13
Fiddle Tunes	14
Blackberry Blossoms	14
Salt Creek	15
Bill Cheathum	16
Fire on the Mountain	17
Devil's Dream	18
Leather Breeches	19
Katy Hill	20
Paddy on the Turnpike	20
Billy In The Lowground	21
Soldier's Joy	22
Ricket's Horn Pipe	23
Florida Blues	24
Peacock Rag	24
Slides and the Key of A	25
12-Bar Blues	26
Slurs and the Key of D	27
12-Bar Blues	27
The Closed Position	28
12-Bar Blues	31
Elementary Double Stops	32
Key of A	32
Sally Goodin	33
12-Bar Blues	34
Key of D	35
Ragtime Annie	35
Key of G	37
12-Bar Blues	38
John Hardy	38
John Henry	39
Key of C	40
Nine Pound Hammer	40
Shady Grove	40
Back Up And Push	41
Key of F	42
Key of E	44
Darling Corey	45
It's Time for The Whippoorwill To Sing	45
Advanced Double Stops	46
Key of A	46
Let Me Rest	46
12-Bar Blues	47
Key of D	48
Little Joe	48
I Won't Be Hanging Around	49
12-Bar Blues	49
Key of G	50
Before I Met You	50
Flowers of Love	50
Key of C	51
On My Mind	52
Careless Love	52
Careless Love	53
Keys of B and B♭	54
You Live In A World All Your Own	54
Sold Down The River	55
The Shuffle	57
Orange Blossom Special	60
Back Up And Push	62
Country Fiddle	63
Crazy Arms	63

INTRODUCTION

The use of the fiddle as a folk instrument is rooted in the traditions of European peasantry. During the Medieval and Renaissance periods secular music was usually structured according to dance forms. The peasants used these forms and integrated them with their own folk melodies; forms such as the reel, square dance, and quadrille evolved from aristocratic counterparts. As the violin developed, it was adopted by both formally trained musicians and the peasants. In the Anglo-Saxon countries the fiddle became an instrument of major importance in the development of the Irish, Scottish and Welsh jiggs, reels and hornpipes.

When the people of these countries migrated to the New World they brought their dances and music with them but, separated from more formal music, the tradition was left to develop without outside influence. An examination of fiddle music can show the effects of environment and geography on this development. The tunes found in New England have an altogether different sound and beat than those of the South; even in the South itself there are many different styles.

After the fiddle was brought to the American continent and became established as a major folk instrument, the number of tunes and dances increased greatly, especially in the South, where the hoedown fiddle reached the peak of its development. The first innovation in the development of fiddle music in the U.S. occurred in the latter half of the 1800's with the advent of the fiddle-banjo duet. Then, in the first decade of the 1900's, the guitar was brought into the southern mountains and began to play an increasingly important role in the growth of fiddle music. This trio of fiddle, banjo, and guitar became the basis for almost all the country bands which developed during the '20's and '30's.

During the early part of the twentieth century, while this music was evolving in the mountains, other popular forms of music such as ragtime and jazz were developing, and they had an effect upon the mountain music, as evidenced in fiddle tunes such as *Ragtime Annie* and *Back Up And Push*. In these same years the recording industry was developing and companies like Bluebird, a subsidiary of the Victor company, sent field teams into the mountains to record old time string bands and make commercial recordings of fiddle tunes. Men like Eck Robertson recorded fiddle tunes that were heard throughout the South. About 1922 Eck recorded many tunes, the most famous of which is *Sally Goodin*. In 1923 the Victor company recorded the first bands, including the Powers family, and Gid Tanner And His *Skillet Lickers*, with Clayton McMichen on fiddle; these recordings had a profound effect on the music of other bands.

At this time in the South, several different styles of fiddling were prevalent. One, which had the most important effect on Bluegrass music, was the Negro blues fiddling, typified by the Mississippi Sheiks in their recording of *Sitting On Top Of The World*. This particular style, predominant in the deep South, especially in Georgia and Florida, affected the fiddling of Chubby Wise, the first bluegrass fiddler. Another style was the old-timey sound of men like Posey Rorer who played with Charlie Poole on his recording of *White House Blues*. On this recording, for the first time, the fiddle was used to play back-up to the vocal part; it did not play the melody line along with the voice, but improvised an accompaniment. Finally, the fiddling of men like Bob Wills, Jimmy Revard, and Arthur Smith developed into what is now called country swing, and is a sound most often found in bands of the Midwest. This style has a modern, jazzy sound far removed from its ancestors, the jigg and reel.

At the end of the 1930's with a great rise in the sale of country music recordings, professionally trained musicians began to venture into the field, and recorded hoedowns and fiddle tunes. The result was a much more polished sound. It was smoother and much more pleasurable to listen to. So, under the influence of these recordings, many people, both professionals and amateurs, took to playing the fiddle.

The bluegrass fiddle sound began to develop with the playing of Leslie Kieth, who worked with the Stanley Brothers, and Tom Magnus and Art Wooton, both of whom played with early Bill Monroe bands. It was not, however, until the Florida fiddler, Chubby Wise, began playing with Bill Monroe that the actual lines for this style were formulated. His style was created mostly by his use of single notes and many bluesy slides. Later fiddlers such as Benny Martin, Paul Warren, and Merle Taylor developed the use of the doublestop in country music fiddling. The fiddle music found in today's bluegrass is a combination of both styles. The degree to which each is used depends upon the fiddler and the artist for whom he is working. Vassar Clements and Bobby Hicks formed one of the finest twin fiddle teams to play for Bill Monroe. Each plays in a bluesy style, and their sound resembles that of Chubby Wise. Jimmy Buchanan, a fiddler who worked for Jim and Jesse McReynolds, used mostly double steps, more in the Benny Martin tradition. Other men such as Kenny Baker, Billy Baker, Herb Hooven, and Gordon Terry combine both techniques to form a middle ground between the two styles. All of these will be explored later.

The role of a fiddler in a bluegrass band can vary greatly. Bill Monroe, who created the style of the music and named it after his home state of Kentucky, began making recordings in 1936. These were vocal duets with his brother Charlie, and the only instruments used were guitar and mandolin. Various additions were made to the band from 1938 to 1945 and it was the last form, employing guitar and bass as a rhythm section, and mandolin, banjo and fiddle as lead instruments which has been maintained by Bill as the standard band. In this combination Bill relies heavily on the fiddle as both a lead and back-up instrument. In his search for new ideas and sounds to incorporate into bluegrass music, Bill has tried many ideas including the addition of electric guitar, organ, and piano, but the same basic structure was always maintained.

MUSICAL TERMINOLOGY

Unfortunately, in writing this book it was impossible, because of the lack of frets on the fingerboard, to use a tablature system. It will be necessary to have a basic reading knowledge of music, so I have presented some of the fundamentals here.

The time value of a note, or its duration, is notated by the shape of the note and its stem: (also true of the rests)

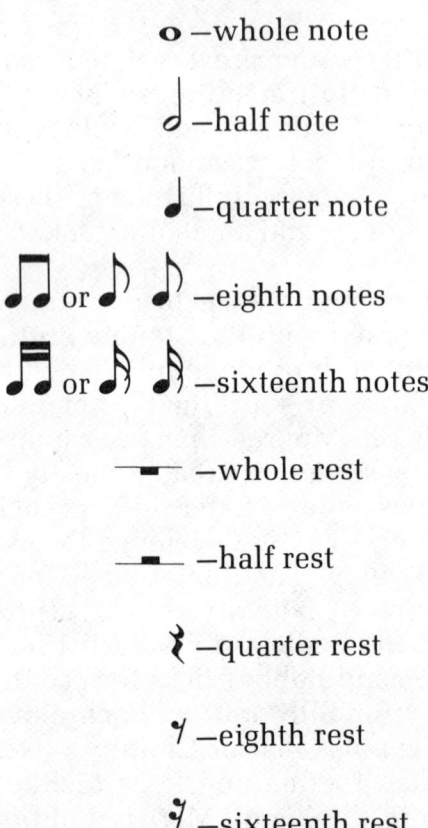

These terms designate the part of a beat or measure they occupy within the time signatures used in this book. The quarter note lasts one beat, the eighth note lasts half a beat and a half note lasts two beats. A dot following a note designates that one half the value of the preceding note is to be added to that note, thus:

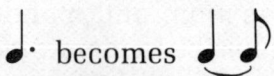

The curved line in the above example is called a tie; it indicates that the value of the two notes is to be added together to make one. It also can be used to indicate a particular bowing; this application will be explained later.

Each line of music is divided into separate units called *measures*, and the measures are separated by a line called a *bar line*:

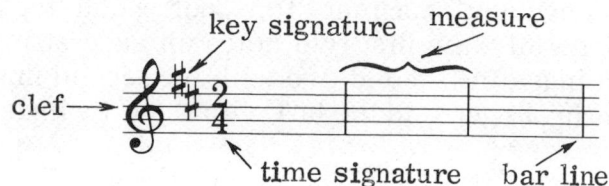

The word *clef* used above refers to a particular range of notes; for our purposes we will be involved with only one, the treble clef. Following the clef sign there are two # markings; this is the key signature and indicates with sharps (#) or flats (♭) which notes are to be raised or lowered a half step. The numbers arranged vertically after the key signature make up the *time signature*. The bottom number indicates the type of note that receives one beat; in this case, the 4 indicates a quarter note. The top number indicates how many beats there are to one measure; in this case there are two.

Gene Lowinger, Bill Monroe, Lamar Greer, Pete Rowan and James Monroe

THE LEFT HAND

Below is a diagram of the fingering on the fiddle. The light vertical lines can be considered imaginary frets, corresponding to those on a mandolin. Generally, the first two notes on each string are played with the first finger, the second two with the second finger, the third two with the ring finger, and the last with the little finger.

E string	F	F#	G	G#	A	B♭	B	C
A string	B♭	B	C	C#	D	D# E♭	E	F
D string	E♭	E	F	F#	G	G# A♭	A	B♭
G string	G#	A	B♭	B	C	C#	D	D#
	1st		2nd		3rd		4th	

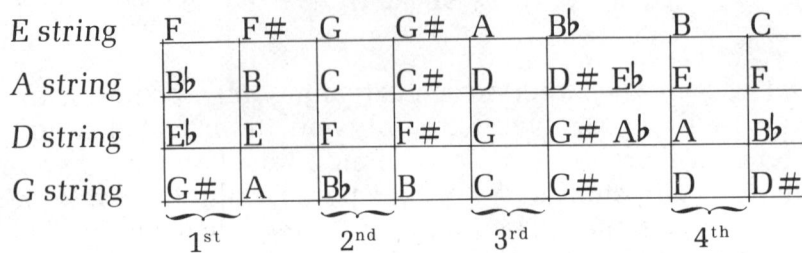

The notes on the music staff are written as follows:

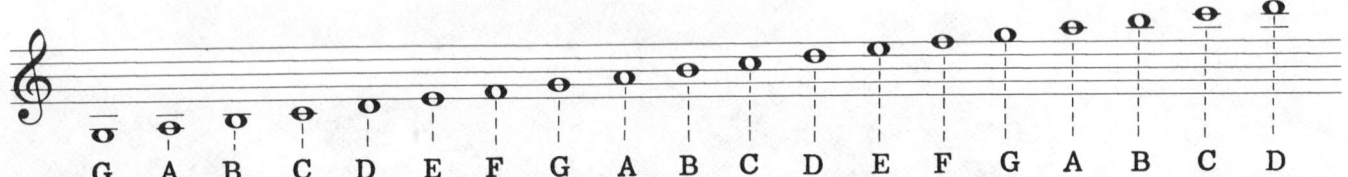

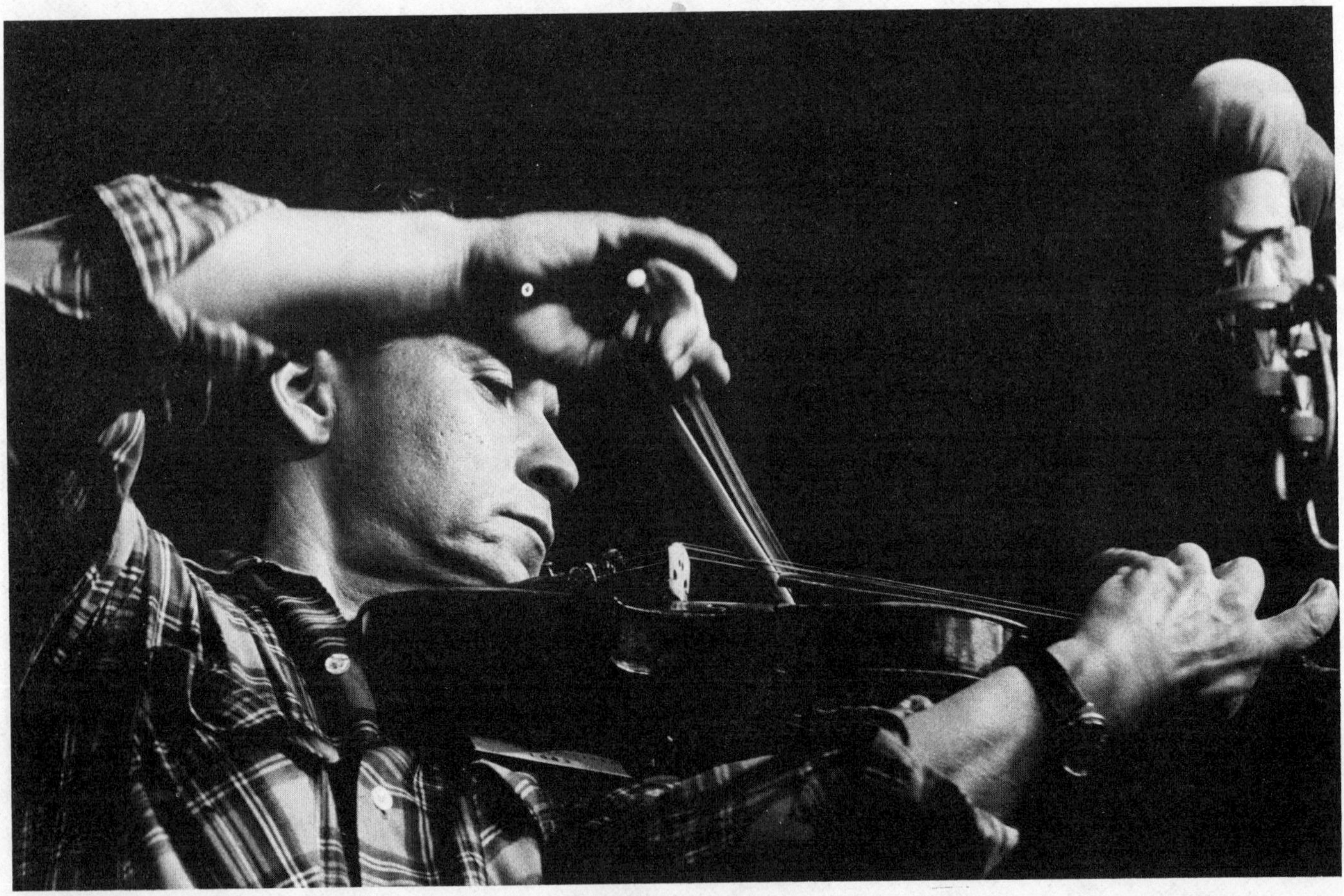

Jean Carignan

In beginning to learn to play the fiddle it would be best to develop the left hand by playing old time fiddle tunes; the music for bluegrass involves more complicated fingerings and rhythms. In the music to follow, a number above or below a note designates which finger of the left hand should be used to play the note; two numbers indicate the best way to play a doublestop.

The proper position for holding the fiddle is the standard position: place it on the left shoulder so that it rests on the collar bone, and place your chin in the chin rest. The neck of the fiddle should be supported only by the thumb, but it is possible to rest it just below the index finger also. *The palm should not be flat against the neck.* Many fiddlers play this way but it decreases finger mobility and speed.

When playing a melodic line in a slow tune it might be desirable to create a sweet singing tone by using a *vibrato*. This technique is very complicated and could take several pages to discuss. By keeping the palm against the neck, vibrato becomes almost impossible to execute. There are three types to be concerned with: finger, wrist and arm vibrato; the best sound is created with a combination of all three, but many people feel comfortable using just one. The finger vibrato originates in the joints of the fingers of the left hand, and is almost inaudible by itself, so it must be used in conjunction with either the arm or wrist vibrato. The wrist vibrato is created by a back and forth (not lateral) motion of the wrist, and the arm vibrato is produced with the same type of motion from the elbow.

 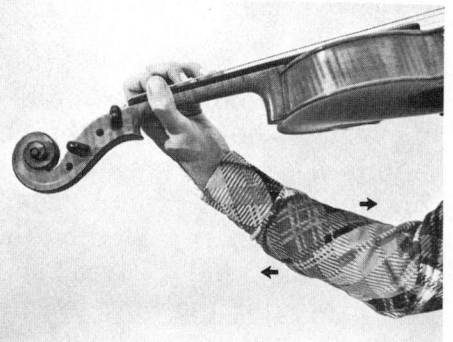

THE RIGHT HAND

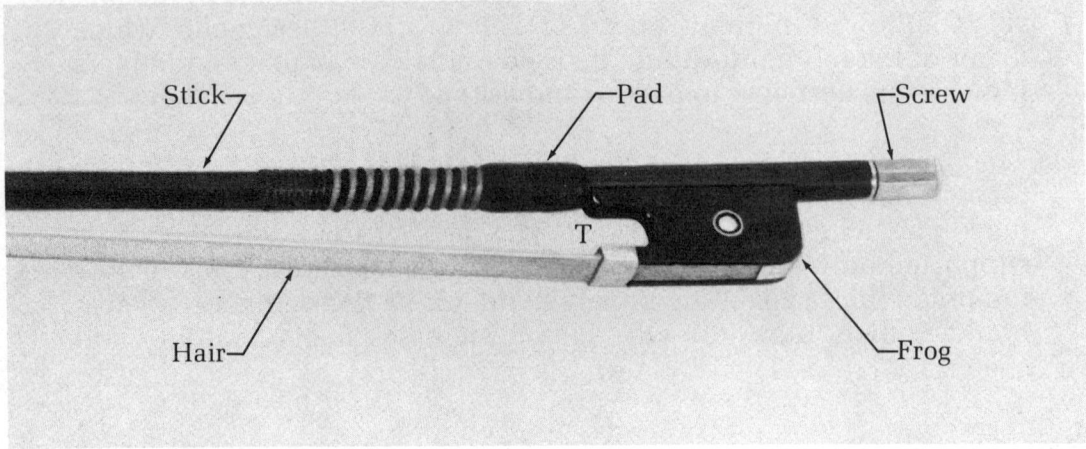

Above is a photograph of the end of the bow which is held in the right hand. The position is designed to give the player the greatest possible balance and control. The tip of the right hand thumb should be placed on the bow stick at the end of the frog (marked with a "T") and should be bent at the knuckle. The index finger is placed on the top of the bow in front of the thumb. The remaining fingers should rest on the bow and the middle finger rests opposite the thumb. Bow pressure can be controlled from this position by adjusting the pressure through the index finger, using the thumb as a fulcrum. It can also be controlled by regulating the amount of weight placed on the bow with the arm.

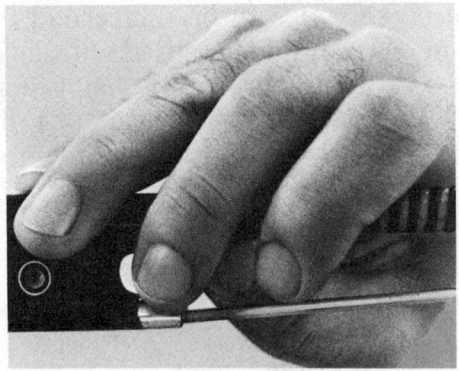

The wrist, elbow and shoulder are the points from which the arm moves the bow across the strings. A vertical motion from these points is used to change the bow from one string to another. In playing upbow, notated as V, the tip of the bow, the end farthest from the right hand, is placed on the string. The elbow should have only a slight bend and the wrist should be level with the knuckles of the hand. Moving the bow up, the elbow should bend, and the wrist should rise above the knuckles.

In playing downbow, notated as ⊓, the forearm should move by unbending at the elbow, while the wrist becomes level with the knuckles.

The motion of the wrist in changing bow direction should be very smooth. A good way of checking to see if everything is moving correctly is to watch in a mirror as the motion is practiced; the bow, as it is drawn, should travel in a line parallel to the bridge. The wrist should be relatively loose; this will help in smoothing the sound and enable you to play faster and with more ease.

The first exercise for bow motion should be repeated on each string. Change the bow direction for each note.

Playing the exercise on the D string, first use separate bows for each note, then slur every two (play two notes in the same bow stroke), then change direction and play the next two in the same bow.

Most fiddlers develop their own patterns for bowing, or use whatever bowing happens to be comfortable for them. Some use no slurs at all on the fast notes of old-time fiddle tunes, but this gives the melody a rough sound. The following is a pattern which will be most adaptable in playing old-time fiddle tunes:

However, the tunes are often comprised of running sixteenth notes; two notes must be slurred into one bow and the next two played separately:

11

Here is the same scale exercise shown before but with the new bowing pattern:

The following tune, *Old Joe Clark*, is simple and follows the pattern shown above. Remember that while learning these tunes you will often find runs adaptable for bluegrass breaks. Those that are most useful have been underlined.

Old Joe Clark

Another bowing pattern which can be used employs the slurring together of every two notes. The accent occurs not on the first note of every group as before, but on the third note as indicated by an accent mark >.

This bowing can be used in tunes such as *Sally Goodin*. It is shown here in conjunction with other patterns.

Sally Goodin

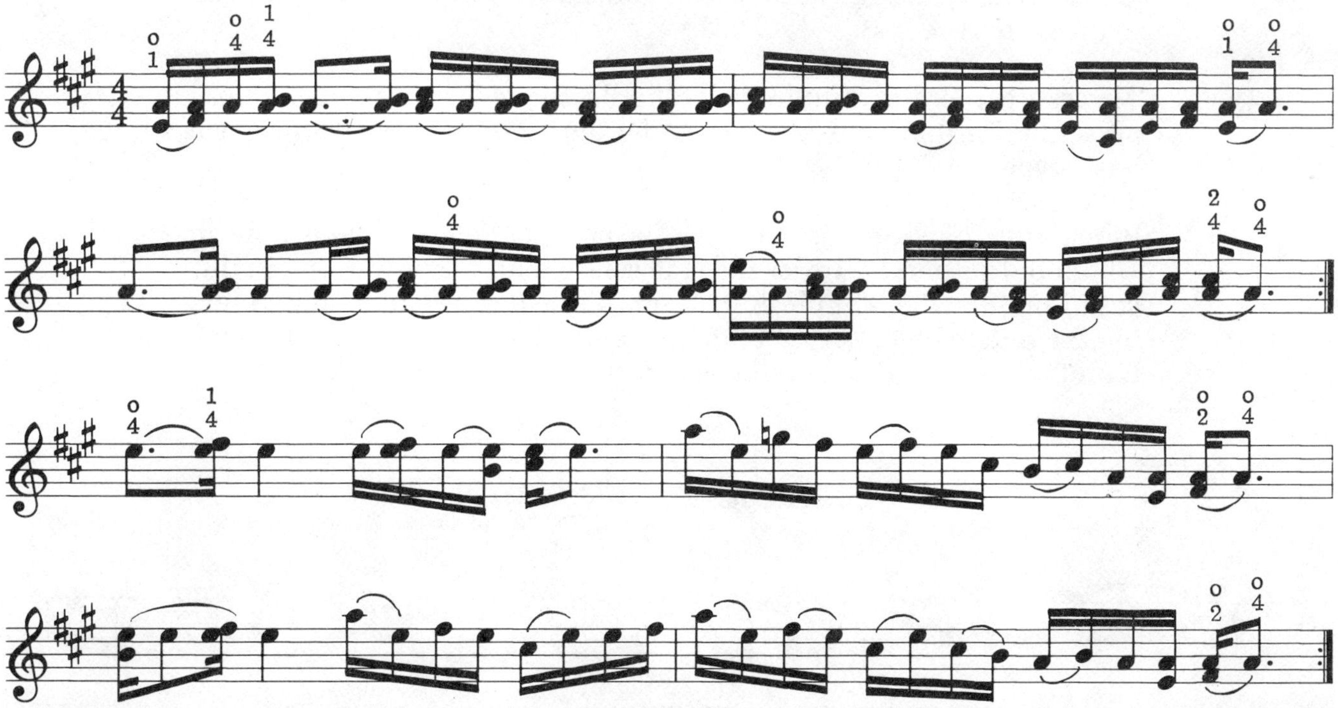

The Oldtimers

FIDDLE TUNES

Fiddle tunes are usually similar in structure. They are divided into two sections of eight measures each; so a whole tune consists of sixteen measures. A common practice in playing these tunes is to go through each section twice before going on, so that a tune is played in the form A-A-B-B.

There are literally hundreds of fiddle tunes in existence. Those presented in this book are either the most common or represent a basic type.

Blackberry Blossoms is typical of a certain type of fiddle tune in which the second half goes into the relative minor of the key, in this case E minor. The doublestops used in this half are played by placing the index finger across both the D and A strings so that you play E on the D string and B on the A string.

Blackberry Blossoms

Several variations can be used for the melody of the first half of this tune. The first is a retrograde of each group of notes:

The next is a series of repeated notes:

The last avoids using the high B altogether:

Salt Creek, an old fiddle tune, was recorded by Bill Monroe and released by Decca on a single (#31596) as a banjo instrumental. Bill Keith played banjo and the fiddle break was done by Kenny Baker, who is one of the best fiddlers to have ever worked for Bill Monroe; his fiddling style is smooth and fluid. This tune is a bit different from the others; the bowing is not as constant and there are some syncopations in the second half. In measures seven and fifteen, a G♯ is used but a G♮ could be substituted to create a more old-timey sound.

Salt Creek

Bill Monroe and Bradford Keith

Copyright © 1963 by Champion Music Corporation, 445 Park Ave., New York 10022. All rights reserved. Used by permission.

The next tune, *Bill Cheathum,* is an old timer that was recorded often by fiddlers and bands in the 1930's and 40's, and more recently by fiddlers such as Tommy Jackson and Gordon Terry. The bowing patterns are more complicated, since they involve both patterns explained in the chapter *The Right Hand* (p.10).

Bill Cheathum

There are several possibilities for variations in the melody. The two shown are just for the first two measures. The first begins with the fourth finger and open E string.

The second begins on the G string and is very similar to the opening of *Salt Creek.*

As in the case above, there will often be chances to substitute or change runs, or *licks* as they are sometimes called, in a tune. Improvising in this way can create an excitement in a tune which might otherwise become monotonous.

The next tune is more of a show piece for the fiddle than a square dance number, although it can serve as either. Usually it is played lightning fast; in fact, that is how it got it's name. While at the Galax Old Fiddler's convention in 1963, an old fiddler, aptly enough, told me that some "feller was playin' this tune so fast that his fiddle caught fire an' set fire to the whole woods." The tune is known by different names such as *Fire On The Mountain*, or, as Joe Maphis, an expert country guitarist calls it, *Fire On The Strings*. It begins in the key of A, but half way through there is a key change and the second part is in D. The last two measures form an ending, sometimes called a *tag*, which moves from D back to A so that the piece can be repeated.

Fire On The Mountain

Devil's Dream was recorded by Bill Monroe and the Bluegrass Boys as a banjo instrumental featuring Bill Keith (Decca #31540). Many Protestant sects forbade dancing and considered it a sin. But in the hands of a good old time fiddler, standing still was often quite difficult because of the rhythm of the music. So the fiddle and the tunes associated with it drove people to dance and became known as the devil's instrument; thus evolved the name of this tune.

Devil's Dream

Bill Monroe

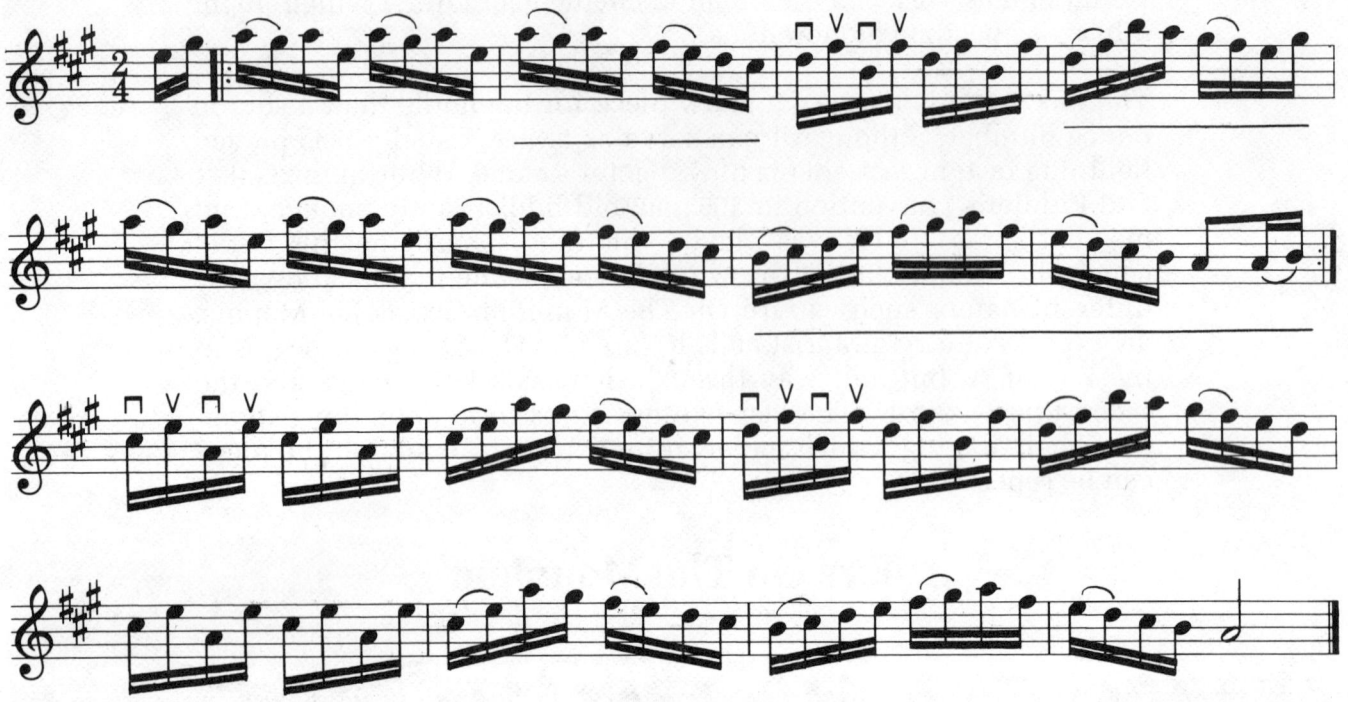

Copyright © 1965 by Champion Music Corporation, 445 Park Ave., New York 10022. All rights reserved. Used by permission.

Because the tune is really quite simple there are many possible variations. In the third and fourth measures you could play:

Or in measures eleven and twelve:

In measures seven and eight, and again in fifteen and sixteen it is possible to play:

The next two tunes are examples of the most common type of fiddle melodies. Harmonically, they are very simple. *Leather Breetches* is a very popular tune in the South; every fiddler has his own version of it.

Leather Breetches

Katy Hill is another fiddle tune which is well-known throughout the South, although it sometimes goes under the name *Sally Johnson*.

Katy Hill

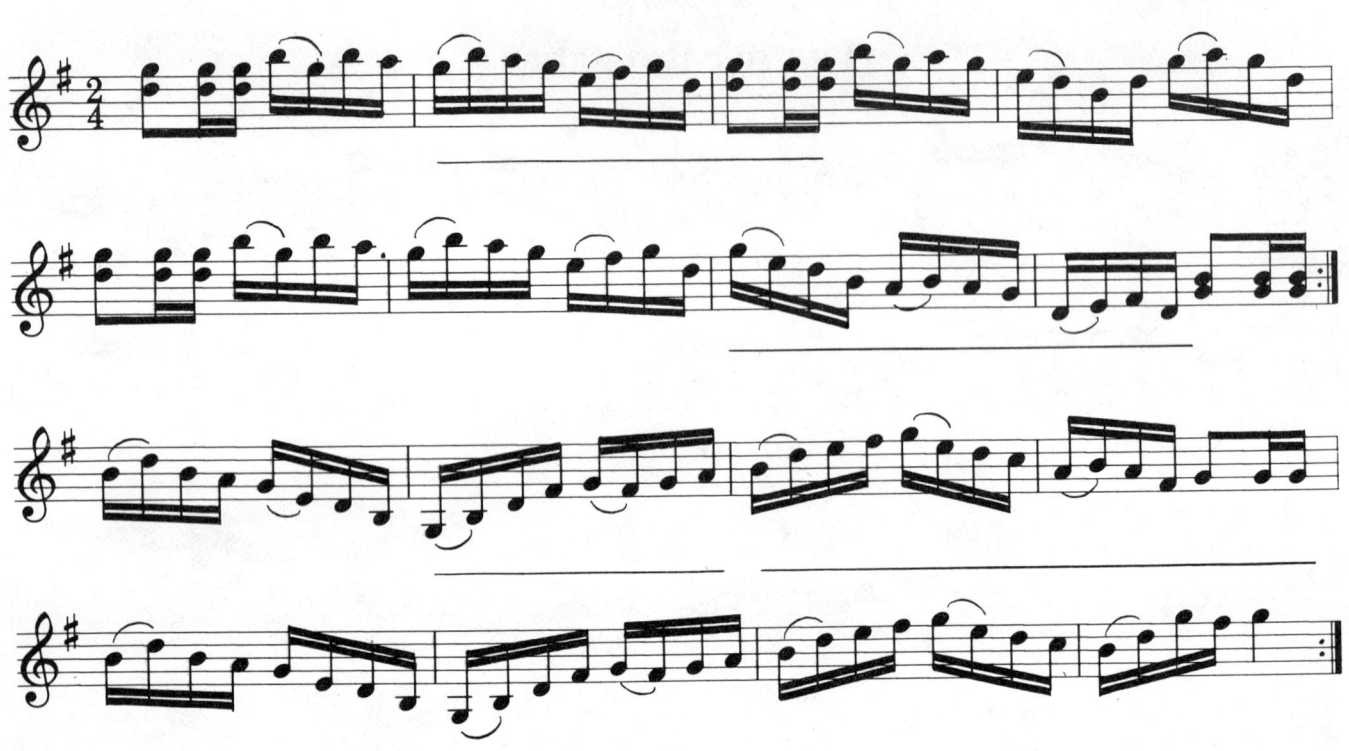

Paddy On The Turnpike is obviously of Irish origin. The tune is harmonically different from the previous ones; it can be best described as *modal*, indicating the use of a chord on the lowered seventh of the scale. In this case, in the key of G, it is the F chord.

Paddy On The Turnpike

Very often in a fiddle tune there is a harmonic movement to the relative minor, as in *Blackberry Blossoms*. In *Billy In The Low Ground* there is a shifting between C major and A minor.

Billy In The Lowground

Soldier's Joy, which is an old-fashioned hoedown that has been adapted to many instruments, is an old Irish reel and also goes under various other names.

Soldier's Joy

This is the original way of playing the first four measures; it can be used as a variation.

The next tune is also of Irish origin. It was originally a hornpipe, a dance which was slower than the reel, had a lot of sycopation, and a heavily accented beat:

When played as a fiddle tune the tempo is faster and both the sycopation and heavy beat are dropped. This is *Ricket's Hornpipe*.

Ricket's Hornpipe

The next two tunes are more modern than those presented so far and are strictly American in origin. They were written by "Old-time" Arthur Smith, whom many people consider to be the king of old-time fiddle playing. One can hear in his playing the roots of modern country fiddling, which served as a starting point for the playing of Chubby Wise and others. The first tune, *Florida Blues*, has a "stomp" feeling to it. There is no set way of bowing these pieces, the one shown might be most comfortable. The arrows above the notes indicate slides to be played on those notes. When the arrow points up, the slide is to be played from below the note to that note; when it points down, the slide is to be played from above to that note.

Florida Blues

Arthur Smith

Copyright © 1944 Berwick Music. All rights reserved. Used by permission.

The second piece is *Peacock Rag*, heavily influenced by the feeling of ragtime. These two tunes could almost be considered country swing melodies; the constant bow patterns and long sixteenth note runs are no longer present. These ideas are much more melodic and lend themselves more easily to improvisation.

Peacock Rag

Arthur Smith

Copyright © 1973 by Glad Music Co. All rights reserved. Used by permission.

Slides and the Key of A

The technique for both hands in playing bluegrass fiddle is more complicated than for old time music. There is more shifting, double-stopping and sliding in the left hand, and bowing patterns are more complex.

Slides occur most commonly on the third of a chord; in the key of A this would be C#:

The bluesy effect can be heightened on some slides by making the third a half step lower (C# to C♮):

The next lick is very common throughout fiddle breaks, and is usually used as a *tag* or ending to a break, but could also be used to fill in gaps in the vocal line when playing back-up behind a singer.

These licks are applicable in many tunes depending on the chord progression. The following is a typical break for a 12-bar blues in the key of A. A great many tunes in Bill Monroe's repertoire follow this chord pattern, so several different versions of 12-bar breaks will be shown in various keys throughout this book.

12-Bar Blues

You can see at the end of this break the previously mentioned tag played one octave lower; in the last full measure another very common tag is used. A break such as this could be used very effectively in a tune like *Heavy Traffic Ahead*, and the various licks and slides might be integrated into a break for *True Life Blues*, both of which are old Bill Monroe tunes.

Bill Monroe and The Bluegrass Boys (with Tex Logan-fiddle and James Monroe-guitar)

Slurs and the Key of D

The use of slurs, or playing several notes in one bow stroke, is a matter of personal taste determined by what phrasing is desired. Following are two examples of licks bowed in various patterns.

These bowing patterns create a flowing type of line which might be desirable in a song like *Sweetheart You've Done Me Wrong*.

The next break is for a 12-bar blues in the key of D, and combines all of the techniques that have been discussed so far. There are many slides and slurs in addition to flatted thirds and sevenths.

12-Bar Blues

Here again, as was the case in the 12-bar blues break for the key of A, is a collection of common licks integrated into one break. Any lick or phrase could be used in many tunes in this key such as a Bill Monroe instrumental called *Bluegrass Special*.

It is possible to apply these licks, and those shown for the key of A, to tunes not in these keys. By moving a lick to the next higher string it is transposed to a key one fifth higher; moving down one string transposes it a fifth lower.

The Closed Position

The closed position is one in which the index finger is placed on the tonic of the key; so in the key of B it would be placed on the note B on the A string. The same is true for the keys of C and B♭. A break which is played in a closed position can be played in any other key by simply placing the index finger on the proper note and working around it. In this way the index finger acts the way a capo would on a guitar or banjo; when used on the A string, the new key is transposed up from the key of A. The second finger plays the notes the index finger would normally play in the key of A, the third finger plays those of the second, and the fourth those of the third. So a figure such as this in the key of A:

would look like this in the key of B:

Similarly, all those licks shown for the key of A can be transposed to the keys of B♭, B, C, and D on the A string, and to E♭, E, and F on the D string. However, you should remember that some of these keys can also employ open strings; these keys will be discussed later.

Goodbye Old Pal was recorded by Bill Monroe twice. The first time was in 1945 with the original Bluegrass Boys (Monroe, Flatt, Scruggs, Chubby Wise). On that particular recording (Harmony HL 7315) the fiddle is the only lead instrument, and the song is in the key of B. The second recording was made in 1957 and appears on a Decca album entitled *Knee Deep in Bluegrass* (Decca #8731). That particular album is interesting because Monroe was in very good voice when he recorded it. *Goodbye Old Pal* was recorded in the key of D. But the album is interesting from another point of view.
Most of the fiddle work on the album is done with twin or triple fiddles, a combination Bill Monroe is very fond of, so much so that he wrote a number of fiddle tunes for two and three fiddle combinations.

The next commonly used licks might be used to good advantage in improvising a break to *Goodbye Old Pal* in the key of B.

The first of these simply moves within a B chord; it might be used to go from the dominant chord (F#) to the tonic. The second involves a double slide on the D# and moves either within the B chord or from B to F#. The third example uses a flatted seventh to heighten the bluesy effect and also employs some very effective syncopations. Example four simply moves within a B chord.

The most common lick used in the closed position is very adaptable to other keys:

It is often used to close a break. The following phrase uses this as a tag. Very often it might be desirable to begin a song with a simple four bar introduction such as this, which is just a combination of licks moving from a B chord to an F# chord and back to B, rather than to play through the whole melody.

The next two licks combined with some of those above could be put together to make a break for a song like *Rose of Old Kentucky* (Harmony HL 7290):

All of these licks can be used in the key of B♭. Although it is not the intention here to present doublestops, the next lick is quite easy to play and can be integrated conveniently into a break when used in conjunction with others shown here.

It moves harmonically from a B♭ to an F chord. The motion from the D to the D♭ is slow, played with the third finger, to create a slide between the two notes, and should sound as though it were leading into the C, played with the second finger.

Bill Monroe's first recording of *Blue Moon Of Kentucky*, which is strictly in $\frac{3}{4}$ time (Harmony HL 7290) is in the key of B♭ and might prove to be an excellent testing ground for all the licks shown for the closed position.

The last examples in this chapter cover the key of C in the closed position. The first lick moves within a C chord and uses a syncopated slide across the bar line.

The second is more syncopated; it is written two different ways to help clarify the rhythm:

In the last example there is a double slide, first *up* to the note, then *down* from it:

These three licks are integrated into the following typical 12-bar blues break.

12-Bar Blues

ELEMENTARY DOUBLE STOPS

The following sections are divided into the various keys one would use in playing bluegrass fiddle. This chapter deals only with basic materials such as the actual double stops, licks which are adaptable to breaks, and simple breaks involving double stops. The next chapter deals with more complicated patterns and breaks.

Key of A

In most instances when playing doublestops in bluegrass fiddle, the lower note is the melody and the upper note the harmony, which can be a third, fourth, fifth, sixth or octave above the melody. There are individual cases where the top may be the melody, however, and these will be pointed out. The three basic chords in the key of A are A, D, and E. In the A chord the three notes with which to form double stops are A, C#, and E. In the D chord they are D, F#, and A, and in the E chord, E, G#, and B. These are the double stop possibilities for each chord:

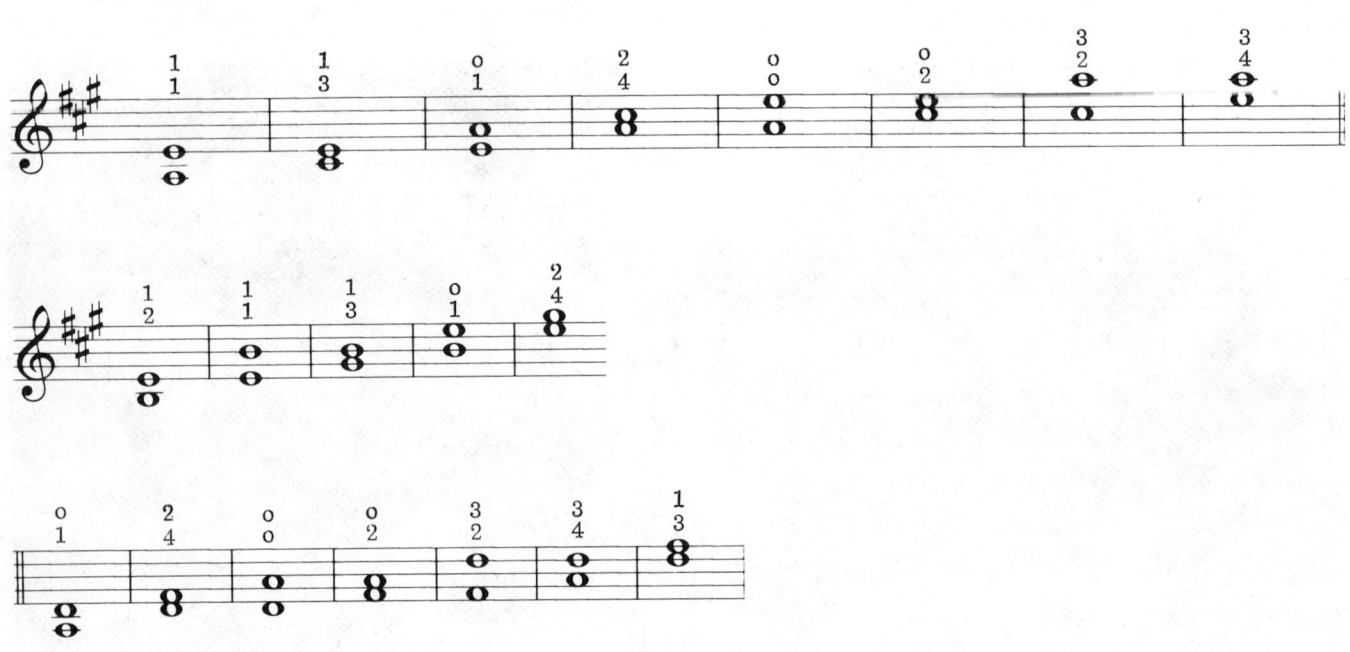

Notice that there are similarities in the finger patterns of each different chord; these make it possible to adapt a lick for one chord to others.

These doublestops can be used in most fiddle tunes in the key of A, such as *Sally Goodin* which was presented earlier, and is shown here in a different version using more double stops.

Sally Goodin

The first lick shown here begins on a unison A played with the open string and fourth finger; the fourth finger then slides down to a G# while the open A is still sounded and in the next measure the G♮ is sounded with the open A string.

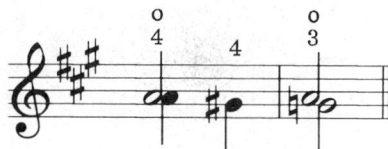

It may be desirable sometimes to slide into a doublestop with either one of the notes or both, which is the case with the next example. The fourth and second fingers simply slide up and down in half steps.

The following break is another 12-bar blues in the key of A:

12-Bar Blues

Pick-ups to a break may be played with doublestops. The following is an example of how to move to the high A. The second half of the example is a very common variation using a triplet on the first note rather than an eighth note.

This next lick moves from an A chord to D. Continue to play the open A string while playing the G with the third finger on the D string.

When playing runs you might want to play doublestops by using the open A, or E string, or by holding down the E on the D string with the first finger while playing on the G string.

Key of D

The three basic chords in the key of D are D, G, and A. Both the A and D chords were covered in the previous section; the notes in the G chord are G, B, and D, and the possible double stops are:

Ragtime Annie, unlike most of the previous fiddle tunes, is strictly American in origin; it was a piano tune which was adapted for the fiddle. The bowing pattern which is peculiar to this piece gives it a bouncy feeling.

Ragtime Annie

This is a variation on the first part of the melody; it might be advisable to study the section on shuffles before attempting to play it, as the bowing is somewhat complicated.

It is possible to construct licks that move around within a chord by simply playing various doublestops within the chord; this device can be used effectively when playing a slow tune with a held note in it. For example:

There are many different combinations and possibilities which you could make up to suit your own purpose and particular melodic line.

Often there will be opportunities to use doublestops when moving from one chord to another such as:

The first examples indicate the movement from a D to a G chord. In the first example, the third finger slides down to a D♭ and the second finger plays C♮. In the third example the movement is from D to A, and the last example moves from A back to D, the same as in the second example but a fifth higher. All these figures can be played in other keys by changing the strings on which they are played; for instance, to play these licks in the key of G, move everything down one string.

Key of G

The basic chords in the key of G are G, C, and D. The notes of the new chord, C, are C, E, and G, and the double stops are:

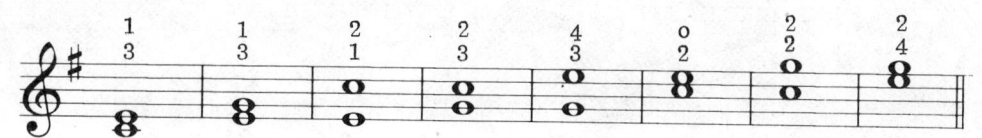

The key of G offers the fiddler a great number of possibilities for integrating doublestops and bluesy slides, especially in songs like *Mule Skinner Blues*, *Girl In The Blue Velvet Band*, and *Can't You Hear Me Calling* (all recorded by Bill Monroe). The first lick below moves within a G chord but uses an F#, which is not a chord tone. This type of slide using fifths creates a special effect, but should only be used in spots where the notes move rather quickly.

The next example moves from a G to a C chord:

This next lick is another special effect, much the same as the first one above; it's played with the first and second fingers sliding from the first to the second doublestop.

All of these licks are shown below along with some very bluesy slides in a 12-bar blues break in G.

12-Bar Blues

Many old time mountain songs can be readily adapted to bluegrass. Songs such as *Pretty Polly, Little Grass of Wine, Little Maggie,* and *John Hardy* have been recorded by the Stanley Brothers, Bill Monroe, and many other bluegrass groups. The next break is for *John Hardy* and integrates a few slides with some doublestops. Here is an exception to a general rule stated before about using a fifth on a held note. In measure seven there is a slide on the B-F#. It should be made slowly so that you don't arrive on the actual note until the second beat of the measure. The greatest effect can be achieved from a break like this by creating the smoothest possible sound, using very connected bow strokes and a vibrato on the held notes.

John Hardy

Throughout most of Bill Monroe's music a fondness for the music of the southern Negro can be heard and felt. In bluegrass style, *John Henry* becomes a fast, hard-driving song. This is the break I used quite often while playing for Monroe. There are several double slides indicated by two arrows above the note, and in a few spots the slides are written out (as in measures 2, 5, and 9). Here again, as was the case in *John Hardy*, the sound should be very smooth and connected.

John Henry

Bill Monroe (with Tex Logan-fiddle)

Key of C

This key was discussed before in using the closed position fingering. Here it is in the open position, and later there will be material which combines both. The chords in this key are C, F, and G. The notes of the F chord are F, A, and C and the double stops are fingered as follows:

A very common lick for both the C and F chord is:

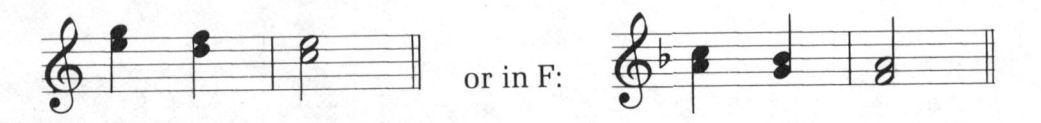

or in F:

Play the first double stop with the first and third fingers, and slide down to the second stop, maintaining the same distance between the fingers.

The break for *Nine Pound Hammer* is really only half of what should be played; this could be repeated again for the second half or you could make up something using sixteenth note runs. On the third beat of the first full measure there is a slide indicated above the E-G; the slide is made with the third finger only (on the E).

Nine Pound Hammer

In the following break for *Shady Grove* an arrow above an E-G doublestop indicates a slide with the third finger only.

Shady Grove

It is also possible to finger the lick so that there is no slide, as shown in the fiddle tune *Back Up And Push*. This is only the first half of the tune; the second part involves shuffling which will be discussed later.

Back Up And Push

Key of F

This key is similar in many ways to the key of C. The basic chords are F, B♭, and C. The notes in the B♭ chord are B♭, D, and F, and the double stop fingering is:

There are two licks which occur constantly in this key: the first can be played with either of two fingerings, depending on whether or not a slide is desired; the second can only be played by changing position.

A common lick which was shown in the last section (key of C) can be used very effectively in the key of F, especially when the slide is used:

Another bluesy, sliding lick which moves within the F chord is:

or in a more complicated form:

After practicing these licks so that they are smooth try throwing in a few doublestops.

or for the second lick:

The following is an eight bar introduction in F using many doublestops; it's in 3/4 time but can be easily adapted to 2/4:

Here is the same break in 2/4:

Key of E

The chords in this key are E, A, and B. The notes of the B chord are B, D#, and F#, and the double stops are:

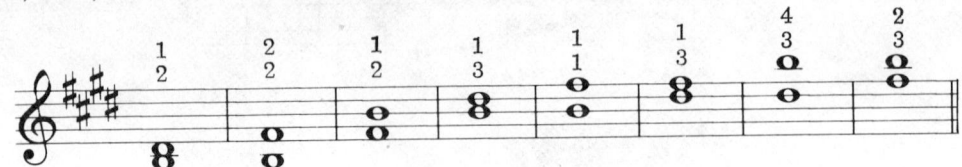

Here are three licks, all basically the same idea, which can be used to either open or close a break.

If a melody note moves from E to G# you could play the E with the fourth finger on the A string and open E string; then add the G# with the second finger on the E string. Try sliding into the E with the fourth finger.

To move from the E chord (E-G#) to A is a simple matter of moving through the flatted seventh which is D♮.

The break to *Darling Corey* as played by Kenny Baker, was taken from a Bill Monroe single (Decca #31596). There are no double stops in it, but there is an important lick which is used.

In the break, Kenny Baker uses a lot of blues slides.

Darling Corey

Bill Monroe

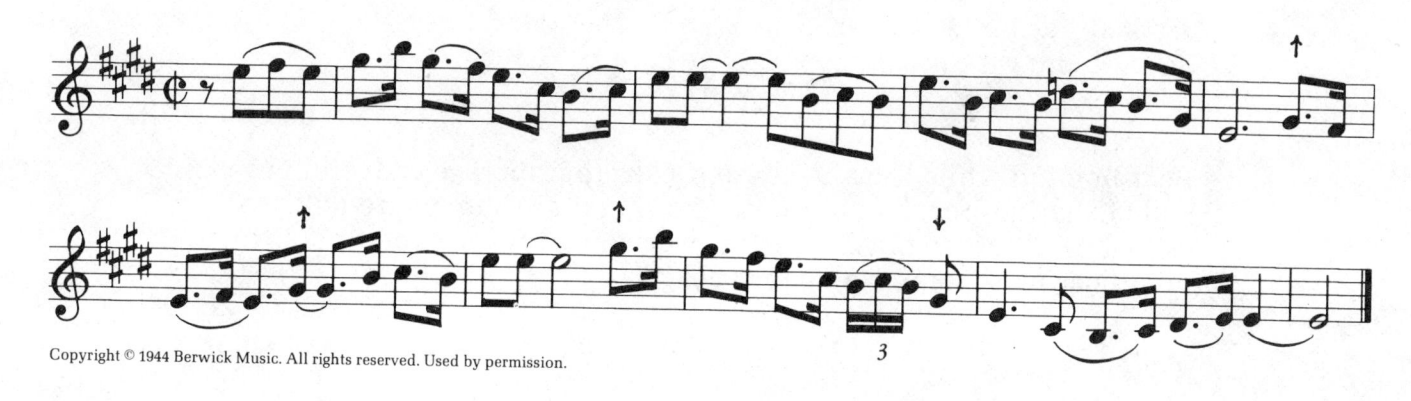

Copyright © 1944 Berwick Music. All rights reserved. Used by permission.

You can increase the sound of the fiddle on a break like this by adding open strings and drone notes.

The last break for this section was recorded by Jimmy Buchannan for Jim and Jesse McReynolds on *When It's Time For The Whippoorwill To Sing* (Epic LN 24031).

When It's Time For The Whippoorwill To Sing

Alton Delmore

Copyright © Renewed 1968 Vidor Publications, Inc. All rights reserved. Used by permission.

45

ADVANCED DOUBLE STOPS

Key of A

Bear in mind while learning these breaks that there are several possible fingerings for double stops. Those that are shown are not necessarily the most convenient for everyone. Try to experiment, to find those most comfortable for you.

Let Me Rest (Decca DL 4537) was played by Kenny Baker for Bill Monroe. In the first measure there are two fingerings shown, to suggest possible variations in fingering.

Let Me Rest

In the fourth measure of the break there is a slide from a G#-B to a B-D; this is not too common a lick, but very effective here because the D acts as the seventh of the E chord. In the last two measures the harmony notes in the double stops occur below the melody. This is a handy device when no other double stop is convenient. Very often, when moving from one chord to another, double stops of this kind can create a pretty effect. The melody note on top can stay the same, while the harmony changes underneath. Examples of this will follow.

The next several licks are commonly found in the key of A. The first can be used when moving from an A to a D chord, the G-B double stop gives the effect of a seventh. This same lick is useable in D if moved down one string, or in E if moved up one.

The following lick can be used to move from an E to an A chord at the end of a break.

However, if you wind up on a low E double stop, the next lick will be more convenient. The slide occurs only on the C#.

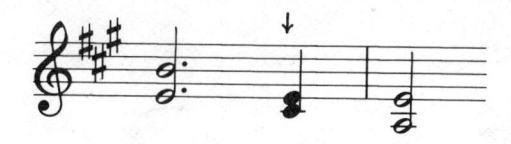

The last break for this key is a 12-bar blues using a very syncopated, swingy type of lick which is played by sliding the first and second finger from the first to the second note.

12-Bar Blues

Key of D

One of the most common licks in this key is:

If it is moved down one string it can be used in the key of G.

Moving to the seventh of a chord before changing harmony has been illustrated in several places already. In the break for *Little Joe*, played by Dale Potter for Bill Monroe, this lick occurs twice; first in the second measure and again in the tenth measure.

Little Joe

Bill Monroe

Copyright © 1961 by Champion Music Corporation, 445 Park Ave., New York 10022. All rights reserved. Used by permission.

Bill Monroe and Kenny Baker

I Won't Be Hanging Around was recorded by fiddler Paul Warren for Lester Flatt and Earl Scruggs. The character is more old-timey than the previous tunes. The first line of music is an introduction to the song, and the second two lines are the break.

I Won't Be Hanging Around

Gladys Stacey, Louise Certain,
Wayne Walker and Marijohn Wilkin

Copyright © 1957 Cedarwood Pub. Co., Inc. All rights reserved. Used by permission.

The following 12-bar blues break is not as rhythmically intricate as was the last one, but it shows very clearly how to move from one chord to another using doublestops.

12-Bar Blues

Key of G

This break to *Before I Met You* was recorded by Paul Warren for Flatt and Scruggs. On the recording, the fiddle shares the break, with the banjo and dobro guitar alternately playing the second half. Shown here are two halves; the first is an introduction to the song and the second is the break.

Before I Met You

Charles L. Seitz, Joe "Cannonball" Lewis
and J. William Denny

Copyright © 1955 Cedarwood Pub. Co., Inc. All rights reserved. Used by permission.

The next passage could serve as an introduction to most slow songs in the key of G. It is written in $\frac{3}{4}$ time, but you can easily adapt it to $\frac{2}{4}$.

It moves first to a C chord, then to a D, and back to G.

This is the same basic type of chord progression used in the next tune, *Flowers of Love*, as recorded by Bill Monroe (Decca DL 74080). The first break is shown as it was recorded:

Flowers of Love

Ellen Martin

The second is an example of the same break using more double stops. The slide in the sixth measure is made only on the D while the G is held.

Copyright © 1962 by Champion Music Corporation, 445 Park Ave., New York 10022. All rights reserved. Used by permission.

Key of C

This key offers a great deal of variety because combinations of both the open and closed positions can be used. The first break is a short introduction which could be used for many songs in this key; it's simple but shows how the open and closed position can be combined. In the third measure there is a double slide on the D. With the second finger, slide up to the note, then slide down from it. The slide on the G in the fourth measure is played by using the third finger in the closed position and sliding to the note from above.

Of the next two examples the first demonstrates how to go to F from C, and the second how to move from there back to C.

To move chromatically from a C to a G chord you could play:

While holding the second finger in place, slide the fourth down a half step. To go from G to C, reverse the lick:

The next break, *On My Mind,* is an example using doublestops only. In some instances there are doublestops where the harmony note occurs below the melody, as in the following lick:

In this case the harmonic motion is from C to G. This same type of figure can be seen in the break.

On My Mind

Tom James and Marijohn Wilkin

[musical notation]

Copyright © 1955 Driftwood Pub. Co., Inc. All rights reserved. Used by permission.

The song was recorded by Flatt and Scruggs. Paul Warren was the fiddler.

In contrast to the last break, the next one does not use many doublestops. *Careless Love* (Decca DL 4382) was recorded by Bill Monroe and the break was played by Kenny Baker.

Careless Love

[musical notation]

Here is another break for the same song using more doublestops.

Careless Love

The next lick is very convenient for moving from a C chord to an F chord, but was not shown in any break.

A variation of this lick combines it with an idea shown in the break for *Little Joe*. After moving to the seventh of the C chord (B♭), another chord tone, G, is played before going to the F-A.

This lick, when moved down one string, can be played in the key of F. It is used by Paul Warren on the Flatt and Scruggs recording of *Dim Lights, Thick Smoke*.

Keys of B and B♭

These keys are the most limited in fiddling and are used often in Bill Monroe's music because they lend themselves well to playing blues. The first break is relatively simple. *You Live In A World All Your Own* (Decca DL 74080) was played by Dale Potter; it's in B major and is an example of how to play double stops within the closed position.

You Live In A World All Your Own

Bill Monroe

Copyright © 1961 by Champion Music Corporation, 445 Park Ave., New York 10022. All rights reserved. Used by permission.

Slides within the doublestops, along with chromatic notes, can heighten blues effects. The repetition of the slide in this lick gives it a very "lonesome" sound:

To move from a B chord to E and maintain this sound, move through the seventh (A♮) chromatically:

and to give the E chord a bluesy sound, move chromatically to its seventh (D♮):

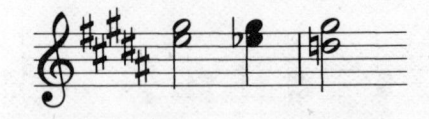

In Dale Potter's break to *Sold Down The River* (Decca DL 74080) doublestops are used sparingly, but both the introduction and break have a very bluesy quality. You can see in the break how effective it is to use the flatted seventh (A♭), and the flatted third (D♭).

Sold Down The River

Vaughn Horton

Intro:

Break:

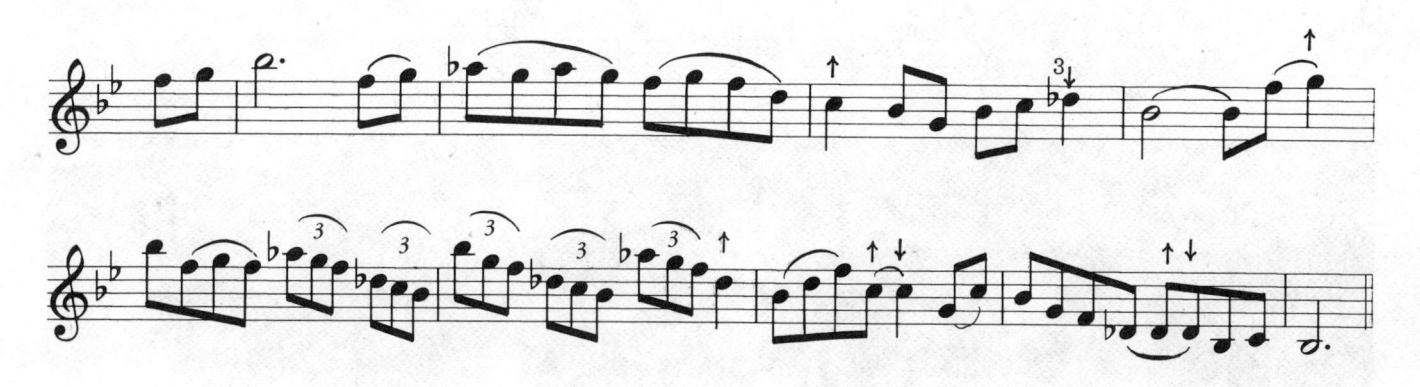

This is also a break for *Sold Down The River,* but I have added more doublestops.

Sold Down The River

Copyright © 1947 Rytvoc Inc. All rights reserved. Used by permission.

The next two licks are very similar. The first goes from a B chord to E then back to B:

The second is the same lick which stays on the E chord:

The last lick begins on a B chord, moves to E and resolves again to B:

The Stanley Brothers and Clinch Mt. Boys

THE SHUFFLE

The shuffle is perhaps the most complicated right hand technique in country fiddling. There are three basic types: the single, double, and triple shuffle. The single shuffle follows the basic rhythmic pattern ♩♫ ; the notation > shows where the accents should be placed. The bow alternates strokes between two or three strings.

The double shuffle is not much more complicated than the single. It follows a rhythmic pattern of ♫♫.

The next shuffle is the most complicated, and it has many variants. The pattern is two measures long, then repeats itself.

This same finger pattern can be used on the D and A strings to shuffle on the E chord. The finger pattern for the D chord is:

When this pattern is moved to the D and A strings, the shuffle can be played in A.

There are many different possibilities for notes to be played with the left hand. The first can be played for an A chord as written, or moved up one string to be played in E. There are two shuffles shown, the second just adds one extra note.

This shuffle, when adapted to the D chord position, is:

When moved up one string this can be played on the A chord.

Another possible shuffle for an E chord is:

[musical notation in 2/4 time, key of E major]

The most popular applications of these shuffles is in the fiddle tune *Orange Blossom Special*. It always has been a past-time of fiddlers to create different types of sounds imitating mules breying, birds singing as in *Listen To The Mocking Bird,* cars and trucks on the highway as in *Lee Highway Blues,* and in this particular case train sounds which make up the first part of the tune. Every fiddler has his own bag of tricks and you should listen to as many different versions as possible to make up your own ideas. The best I have ever heard was played by Richard Greene, a fiddler who worked for Bill Monroe. A few licks are shown here but they are only the easiest and most common.

To imitate the sound of a train whistle various combinations of doublestops on the E chord can be played:

[three musical examples showing doublestop combinations]

You can create the impression of a bell ringing by plucking the E string with your fourth finger (left hand), even while playing any of the above licks.

There are two possible ways of making a sound of a train starting off. The first is to play:

[musical notation example]

Start off slowly at first and gradually get faster to give the impression of building up speed.

The second way is much more difficult to explain. With the left hand hold down the notes G# on the D string and B on the E string. Slide the bow without any pressure, so that the strings don't really sound, from the area of the bridge where you would normally play down towards the peghead of the fiddle, and back up again; both strokes are on the D and A strings. Then cross strings to the A and E and repeat the same motion. As before, start out slowly and gradually get faster.

59

This is the actual fiddle tune. The asterisk six measures before the end indicates the point at which another lick may be substituted. More on that later.

Orange Blossom Special

Ervin T. Rouse

Copyright © 1938, 1956, 1965 by MCA Music, A Division of MCA, Inc. 445 Park Ave., New York 10022. All rights reserved. Used by permission.

After you have played the melody through, go back to E major and play more train imitations, then, when playing the first two measures, pick up the tempo; repeat this each time until it is ridiculously fast or until your arm falls off. Then you are ready to play the classic ending to all fiddle tunes—there are many variations on the *Shave and a Haircut Two Bits* lick. This is one I used most often.

In the key of C there are several shuffle possibilities:

which if moved down one string can be used for F. The next is for G, which can also be for C if moved down.

The use of the shuffle need not be limited to using double stops. It can be used in a break for a song by playing single notes; in this respect the use of the shuffle is bounded only by one's imagination. The following are two examples in B major; the first is on a B chord and the second is for F#.

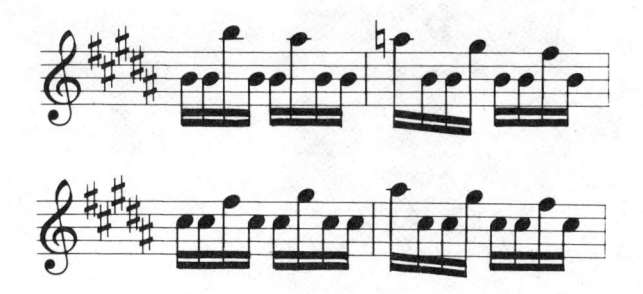

The following shuffle can be substituted in *Orange Blossom Special* at the point indicated by the asterisk.

61

The last shuffle is the second half of the fiddle tune *Back Up And Push* (p. 41). It's repeated twice then the first half is played again.

Back Up And Push

COUNTRY FIDDLE

The differences in fiddle technique between country and bluegrass music become quite obvious upon examination of the type of fiddling done by the musicians in the Ray Price or Buck Owens groups. It consists mostly of single note work using no slides and considerably fewer blues notes. The basic ideas change little from piece to piece because the tempo changes are not as drastic as in bluegrass, and because the role of the fiddle in the band is greatly reduced; in most cases it is nonexistent.

The best example of this type of fiddling can be found in early Ray Price recordings in which Tommy Jackson was the fiddler. One of the simplest elements in all breaks is the beginning; it usually is one of three patterns:

The second most recurrent pattern is the use of a scale run to lead into a melody note. The actual notes depend upon the melody and the harmony; for example, if the melody note is a G:

The first could be used with a G or E minor chord, the second with a C chord.

Two rhythmic patterns return constantly; the triplet is used either as a turn or a scale:

and a dotted rhythm is used to give a bouncy feeling:

The following is a break taken from a Ray Price album (Columbia CL 1566); the fiddler is Tommy Jackson.

Crazy Arms

Chuck Seals and Ralph Mooney

Copyright © 1956 by Champion Music Corporation and Pamper Music, Inc., N.Y. Sole Selling Agent MCA Music, A Division of MCA, Inc., 445 Park Ave., New York 10022. All rights reserved. Used by permission.

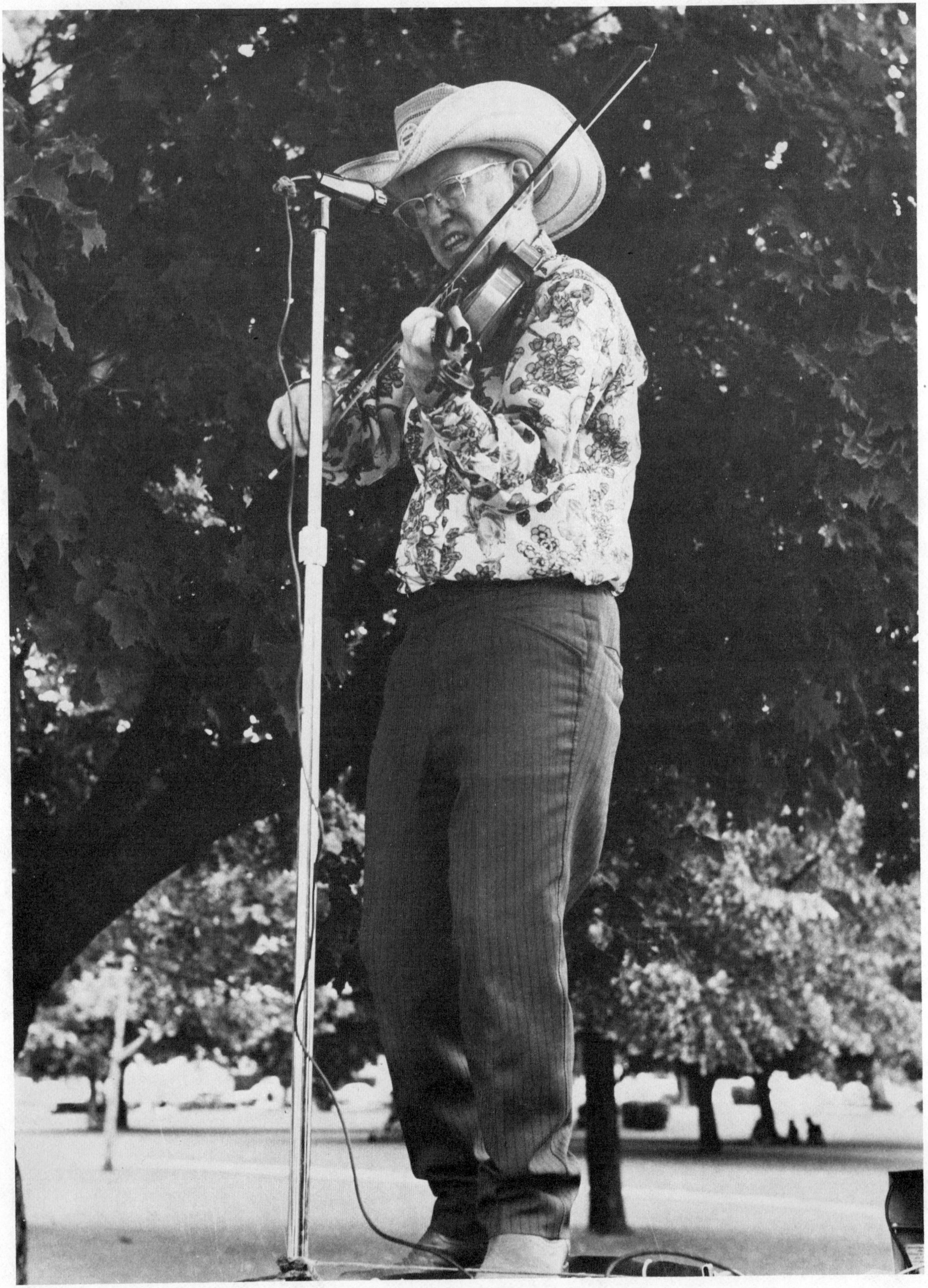